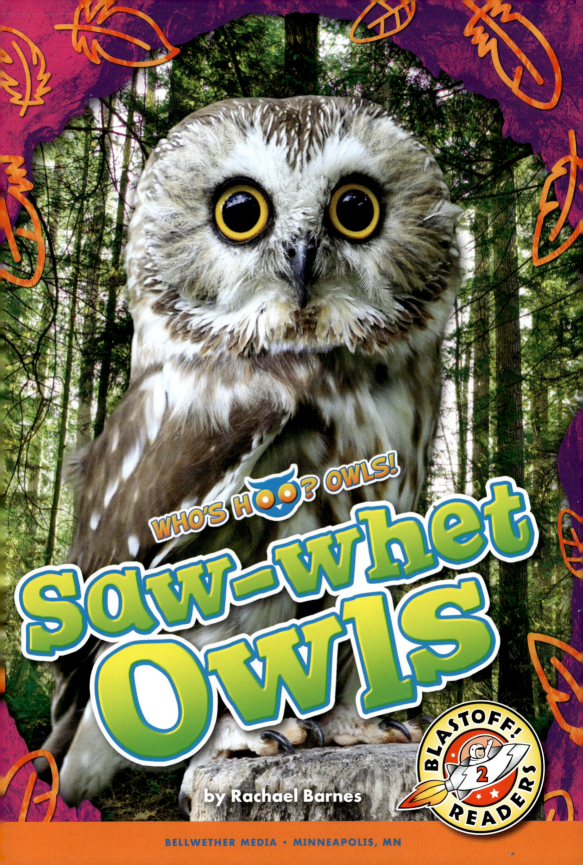

WHO'S HOO? OWLS!

Saw-whet Owls

by Rachael Barnes

BELLWETHER MEDIA • MINNEAPOLIS, MN

Blastoff! Readers are carefully developed by literacy experts to build reading stamina and move students toward fluency by combining standards-based content with developmentally appropriate text.

LEVELS

 Level 1 provides the most support through repetition of high-frequency words, light text, predictable sentence patterns, and strong visual support.

 Level 2 offers early readers a bit more challenge through varied sentences, increased text load, and text-supportive special features.

 Level 3 advances early-fluent readers toward fluency through increased text load, less reliance on photos, advancing concepts, longer sentences, and more complex special features.

★ **Blastoff! Universe**

Reading Level

 Grade K →   Grades 1–3 →   Grade 4

This edition first published in 2025 by Bellwether Media, Inc.

No part of this publication may be reproduced in whole or in part without written permission of the publisher. For information regarding permission, write to Bellwether Media, Inc., Attention: Permissions Department, 6012 Blue Circle Drive, Minnetonka, MN 55343.

Library of Congress Cataloging-in-Publication Data

LC record for Saw-whet Owls available at: https://lccn.loc.gov/2024000764

Text copyright © 2025 by Bellwether Media, Inc. BLASTOFF! READERS and associated logos are trademarks and/or registered trademarks of Bellwether Media, Inc. Bellwether Media is a division of Chrysalis Education Group.

Editor: Christina Leaf   Series Designer: Brittany McIntosh   Book Designer: Veah Demmin

Printed in the United States of America, North Mankato, MN.

Table of Contents

Tiny Too-too-too	4
A Night Owl	12
Life of a Saw-whet Owl	18
Glossary	22
To Learn More	23
Index	24

Tiny Too-too-too

Saw-whet owls are found in many parts of North America. They live in forests.

They are known for their one-note *too-too-too* call.

Northern Saw-whet Owl Range Map

range =

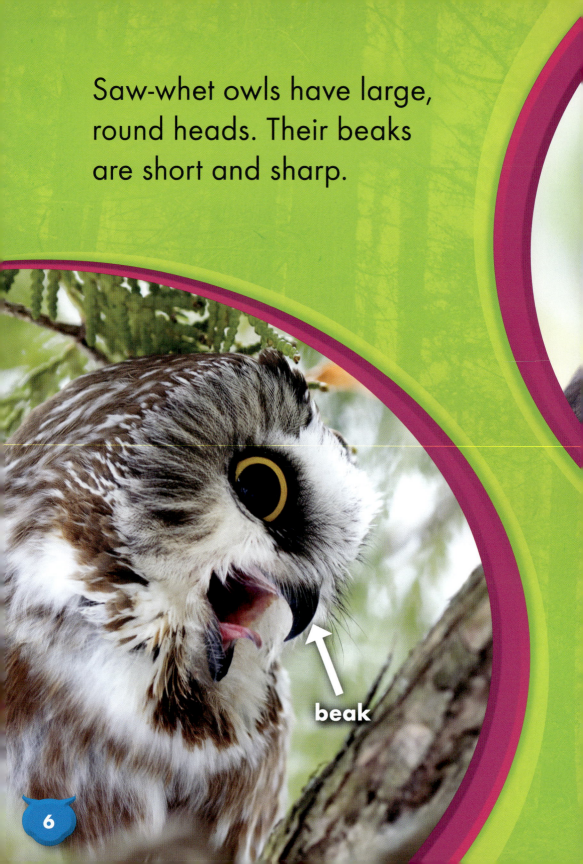

Saw-whet owls have large, round heads. Their beaks are short and sharp.

beak

They have big yellow eyes.
In between them, white feathers form a V shape.

facial disk

The owls' heads and wings are brown with white spots. Their **facial disks** have lighter feathers.

Brown and white feathers fill their chests.

Spot a Saw-whet Owl!

- white V on face
- big yellow eyes
- large, round head

Saw-whet owls are tiny. Their **wingspan** is around 19 inches (48 centimeters) wide.

Adults only grow to about 8 inches (20 centimeters) tall!

Saw-whet Owl Wingspan

0   10 inches   20 inches

around 19 inches (48 centimeters) wide

A Night Owl

Saw-whet owls are active at night. They can hunt in almost total darkness.

Their facial disks help them hear their **prey**.

prey

perch

talon

Saw-whet owls often hunt by swooping down from low **perches**. Sometimes they jump on their prey!

Saw-whet Owl Food

rodents   birds   large bugs

They catch **rodents**, birds, and large bugs with their sharp **talons**.

Saw-whet owls hide from larger **raptors** to stay safe.

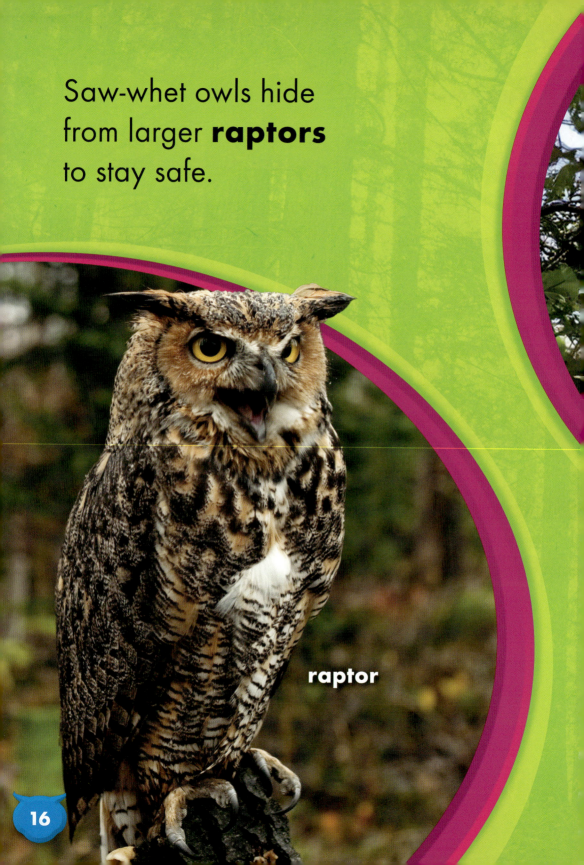

raptor

They rest on low, thickly covered branches. Their feathers blend in with the trees.

Life of a Saw-whet Owl

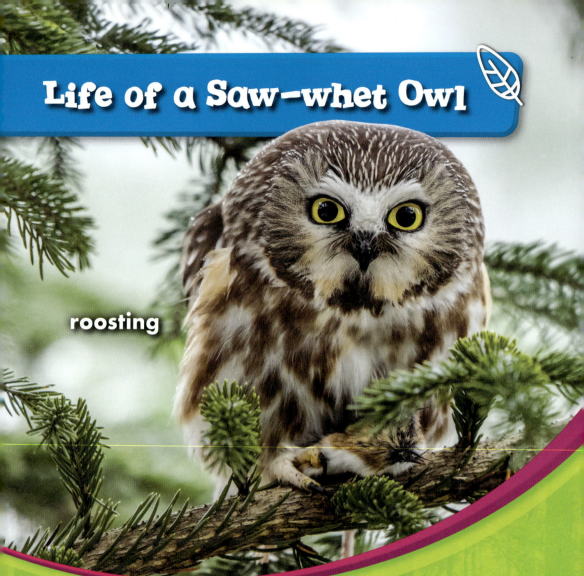

roosting

Saw-whet owls often **roost** in pine trees. They use tree holes as nests.

Some **migrate** in the fall. They move to find food.

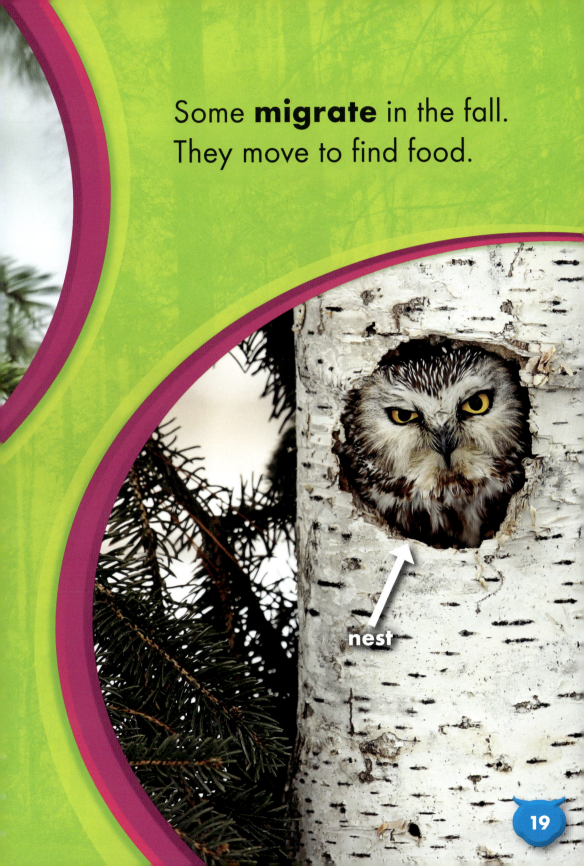

nest

Female saw-whet owls lay around six eggs at a time. Soon, **owlets** break out of the eggs.

Owlets become **fledglings**. One-year-old owls have all of their adult feathers!

fledglings

Growing Up

1. egg — around 1 month
2. owlet — 4 to 5 weeks
3. fledgling — around 1 month

life span: up to 9 years

Glossary

facial disks—the feathers that cover owls' faces

fledglings—young owls that have feathers for flight

migrate—to travel from one place to another, often with the seasons

owlets—baby owls

perches—places to sit or rest above the ground

prey—animals that are hunted by other animals for food

raptors—birds that hunt other animals; raptors have excellent eyesight and powerful talons.

rodents—small animals that gnaw on their food; mice, rats, and squirrels are all rodents.

roost—to rest or sleep

talons—the strong, sharp claws of owls and other raptors

wingspan—the distance from the tip of one wing to the tip of the other wing

To Learn More

AT THE LIBRARY

Kenney, Karen Latchana. *Forests*. Minneapolis, Minn.: Bellwether Media, 2022.

Neuenfeldt, Elizabeth. *Elf Owls*. Minneapolis, Minn.: Bellwether Media, 2024.

Whipple, Annette. *Whooo Knew? The Truth About Owls*. New York, N.Y.: Reycraft Books, 2020.

ON THE WEB

FACTSURFER

Factsurfer.com gives you a safe, fun way to find more information.

1. Go to www.factsurfer.com.

2. Enter "saw-whet owls" into the search box and click 🔍.

3. Select your book cover to see a list of related content.

Index

beaks, 6
call, 5
colors, 7, 8, 9
eggs, 20
eyes, 7, 9
facial disks, 8, 12
feathers, 7, 8, 9, 17, 20
females, 20
fledglings, 20
food, 15, 19
forests, 4
growing up, 21
heads, 6, 8, 9
hide, 16
hunt, 12, 14
jump, 14
migrate, 19

nests, 18, 19
night, 12
North America, 4
owlets, 20
perches, 14
prey, 12, 13, 14
range, 4, 5
raptors, 16
roost, 18
size, 10, 11
talons, 14, 15
trees, 17, 18
wings, 8, 10
wingspan, 10, 11

The images in this book are reproduced through the courtesy of: Erica Ruth Neubauer, front cover (saw-whet owl); Roxana Gonzalez, background; mlorenz, pp. 3, 9; Veronica Phillips, p. 4; Jim Cumming, p. 6; FotoRequest, p. 7; Glass and Nature, pp. 8, 17; Todd Maertz, p. 10; Joe McDonald / The Image Bank / Getty Images, pp. 11, 12-13; Ken Duffney, p. 12; yongsheng chen, pp. 14-15, 18; jitkagold, p. 15 (rodents); punkbirdr, p. 15 (birds); Paul Reeves Photography, p. 15 (large bugs); Martin Prochazkacz, p. 16; critterbiz, p. 19; sam may / Flickr (CC BY 2.0 DEED / Attribution 2.0 Generic), p. 20; Ivan Deng, pp. 20-21; Scott Rashid / Colorado Avian Research and Rehabilitation Institute, p. 21 (egg); All Canada Photos / Alamy Stock Photo, p. 21 (owlet); Sara Tehranian, p. 21 (fledgling); mlorenz, p. 23.